Francisco Marco-Serrano

Making sense of social media ROI

A short guide focused on sales, marketing and strategy

Business Research & Applications Limited

First edition: February 2014
ISBN:1495394026
ISBN-13:978-1495394027

Preface

When my friend Benet Marcos, from Socialancer.com, asked me four years ago to prepare a postgraduate course about the ROI of social media I could not believe this was going to be taking so much time of my life.

It was not the case of me considering the topic was not interesting or it lacked appeal for a quantitative economist as I like to define myself, but I though it would be doing a friend a favour. Nowadays I do not think he realises he is the one that did me a favour unveiling to me so important subject for marketers, communication professionals, and business people in general. Actually, it is important to anyone using social media as a business channel, or considering using it; if you are going to invest some resources into social media, even if it is going to be your own time, you should estimate the returns. Otherwise, you are being dishonest to yourself, or even worse, to your clients or boss.

I come from academia, and I have written some scholarly papers and books; however, when I faced the possibility of writing about social media ROI I though the target reader should not have many time for reading about it, he would want to have a quick guide, or even he would be used to read short guides. These considerations, together with the fact that I wanted to produce something I could release like "yesterday", induced me to write it in an essay form. Hopefully, if you like it, I would consider expanding it; have a good read!

London, 10th February 2014 *Francisco* Marco-Serrano

Contents

Chapter 1
Basics for understanding ROI in social media

1.1 How social media can create value

"Generate value" may be considered as one of the old new adages for company growth. If you are capable of creating value, more people will be willing to buy your product and your revenue will grow. Although you may be thinking it is an empty speech, actually generating value is something achievable and a real driver for company success.

In order to let you understand the concept, how social media can play an important role in leveraging value, and be able to put it into practice I am going to explain you the company's value chain model, how social media can help you create value, and which tool you can start using to spot value creation opportunities.

If you do not provide value to your customers your company will disappear. This is true; those companies that are incapable of adding value for their customers or users are condemned to bankruptcy. Would you buy something that would not bring you any benefit?

When you are setting the price of your product or service think of the value your client obtains. Who is buying your brand? How much is he paying for it? The value for your client is in line with these questions. Value is a concept you have to consider from a customer's point of view: how much would your customer be willing to pay you for getting your product? That is the value of your product! This is, your customer is the one who has the say about the value of your product.

From here, I know what you think the problem is: your customer will not tell you which is the actual value he obtains from your product. The only approximation you have is that is he is buying it, then his value is at least the same as the market price. If you knew the client's value you would be trying to increase the price to approach customer's value.

Further, there is another variable to consider: your cost. Obviously, you will not set a price which is lower than the cost, or your value (profit) will be negative (a loss). However, you have to focus on the customer's value! Basically, it is where your success will reside: set a price above his perceived value and he will not buy;

have an excessive cost and you will need to set a higher price risking exceeding your customer's value and, again, you will sell nothing.

Hopefully, social media can be your ally for avoiding this situation. Although it is totally stupid to try arguing that social media is your medicine (some snake-oil sellers will try to convince you of the opposite), it does make sense to use social media marketing as a tool to improve the gap between your internal cost, the selling price, and the perceived value.

Before you start considering social media, as you would do with some other tools or new activities to drive growth, you need to analyse your business. You should find out where the problem is before knowing how to solve it. One of the methodologies that has been used to analyse where value comes from in a company is Porter's value chain model.

The company's activities can be divided into:

- Primary; logistics and operations, marketing and sales, and service.
- Support; firm infrastructure, human resources management, technology, and procurement.

When you start analysing a company using this tool you realise that the value proposition and the value generation comes from the whole of the organisation; every single member or function should be focused on either increase the perceived value or to reduce the cost, so then, increasing the value. With this in mind, social media can assist you at least in three ways: market research, branding, and internal communication.

Then, what?: Sure! You need a guidance. Along the years many different tools have been developed that embrace Porter's ideas while making the model approachable and usable in practice. One of the best ones is the "Business Model Canvas", which allows to map the way a business model adds value for the customer as the backbone of the company strategy. Along it, you will need to explore the key partners, activities and resources of your business plan, your customer relationships, segments, and channels; of course, you will need to review your cost structure and revenue streams, too.

Guess what? The journey represented by exploring your business plan will help you determine where social media can either offer you extra benefits or cost reductions.

1.2 Why you should measure your social media ROI

Are you one of those professionals who is being continuously asked by many clients or even his boss to calculate the social media ROI? The use of the term social media ROI has been climbing up to become part of the concepts that every social media professional knows (or should know).

It is not rare when reading about digital marketing to find mention of the term. But calculating it just because we are being asked it is quite sad. Do you have any real and powerful reason to calculate it, beyond the solely reason of following a fad? Well, to be honest, I think you should be doing it; here are three reasons to help you convince yourself, your clients or your boss about the importance of the social media marketing.

Learn to manage your resources

One of the rules of management is that you cannot manage what you do not measure. Many people will tell you that measuring only the "soft indicators" (fans, likes, followers.....) you should have enough. That's wrong; you must learn how to measure conversions that occur from these "soft indicators" (those measured in currency I call them "hard indicators"). Whenever you were able to do it, you will know your true ROI. Since this concept is what tells you how much net profit you get from the use of your resources (time and money, primarily), you can learn to manage it; for instance:

- Abandon campaigns that have no return,
- serve as an incentive to analyse why they are failing, or
- you can enhance campaigns that get higher returns.

Show the profitability to your boss or client

Maybe your boss or your client have been seduced by the fashion frenzy of wanting to know the ROI of their social media campaigns. Try to find out if this is the case, and then investigate whether they are also measuring the ROI of other (traditional) media campaigns (radio spots, newspaper ads, yellow pages, etc..), and even if they know the profitability of the latest summer campaign discounts. If they do, it means that your boss or your client manages (or wants to manage) his resources, as I indicated in the previous section.

If he is also sharing ROI information from other channels and campaigns, great! You will have information to know if you are in the right track in the use of social media (your job is generating returns higher or lower than your boss or clients are expecting?).

Moreover, if you had this information before the season, you could even perform a preliminary analysis estimating financial goals matching the other channels in terms of profitability. If it turns out that your boss or client has no idea of what social media ROI is, explain what ROI is and how it can be calculated. Explain to him that not only can be calculated for Social Media, and tell if you obtain the ROI of all marketing channels and projects, then he would learn to better manage their resources (yes, the first point).

Demonstrate the value of social media

In an environment in which there are more and more trouble for getting financing, in the companies there are internal battles for the distribution of budgets between departments. You should use all available weapons. The"YOU need to be in social Media" is no longer valid as the value proposition. With this sentence you may get some short term client or convince your boss to let you open a new social media marketing campaign….. but in the long run you will see that the ploy will drain; figures must convince, although not any number; guess which one: ROI!

Indeed, profitability is a standard indicator that any director, manager, chief financial officer, marketing or business will understand. Why should you assign funds to carry out a campaign in social media when they can be used to offer trade discounts?, or will investing in a brand new machine bring more value to the company than if you increase your budget for social media campaigns? Yes, the only way you will be able to compare these three actions will be analysing your results in the form of ROI.

Finally, you will have noticed that this trinity of ROI is actually one single reason, focused on the value of social media. Our battle is for everyone to be able to speak the same language, because now marketers talk about fans, while business and financial professional talk about money. Honestly, I see more viable than all learn to speak in terms of money (who does not like money?). The translation process is not simple, and requires a lot of work….. but it is the way you have to follow.

1.3 How to apply the Balanced Scorecard to your social media strategy

Do you know the "old" strategic models can be used to design and monitor your social media strategy? There are other newer models that could be used, as well; for instance, the above-mentioned "Business Model Canvas". However, I am going to focus on an "oldie": the "Balanced Scorecard".

More than twenty years ago, Kaplan and Norton led a research project that aimed at finding new ways of measuring and monitoring the results of the strategy deployment in the company from a multidimensional perspective. They were looking to escape the at the time practice of focusing too much on just financial indicators. The Balanced Scorecard (BSc) is a tool for deploying and monitoring the strategy. It takes into account four different types of indicators: financial, customers, internal processes, and learning and growth.

These four perspectives or groups of indicators are filled with contents by means of the definition of key performance indicators (KPIs), which are a translation of the the vision and mission of the company. Further, there must be a cause-effect relationships structure that links all the KPIs along the four different perspectives.

To integrate social media into the company strategy you can use the BSc as a design tool. First, you should start from the Social Media Plan, which is the document that summarises the strategic behavior of the company in the social channels; it should be aligned with the general strategy of the company. If both the Social Media Plan and the general strategy share the same general goals, both are already integrated: well done, this is how it should be. If they are not aligned we are facing what it is called strategic dissonance, and you have to aim for sorting that problem out. How could you integrate social media within your corporate strategy in an efficient way?

We recommend creating a new perspective: Internet. Then, by applying the BSc tool with the four plus one perspectives, you will be able to map your strategy linking the different KPIs for customers, financial, internal and learning, to those from the internet perspective.

1.4 Nine areas of your business you should empower using social media

Generating value is not a new concept or a trend that will vanish along the following months. Value is what drives your customers to buy from you. The problem you may face is understanding it within the usage of social media. Actually, even the most advanced marketers and strategists are having to test-test-test in order to extract the maximum of the new media channels. To speed up the learning process of those already testing I am going to introduce you to: the value chain in the company, the "Business Model Canvas" as a tool to analyse your value generation, and how to create value with social media.

According to Michael Porter, internet has improved the speed of transmission of information, interlinkage, and its diffusion in real-time along the full value chain. Internet first, and the social networking sites now, have achieved the availability of more and better information that allows companies to optimise both the primary activities (i.e.manufacturing) and the support ones (i.e.procurement). Wealth and quality of information are allowing us to improve the productivity and efficiency of our processes and resources.

The "Business Model Canvas" is a simple but powerful methodology to explain, analyse, and develop your business strategy. The authors, Alexander Osterwalder and Yves Pigneur, propose a canvas-style representation of the business model which dissects the value chain of an organisation into nine sections: key partners, key activities, key resources, value proposition, customer relationship, channels, customer segments, cost structure, and revenue streams.

If you are willing to use this model for designing your social media strategy let me recommend you the following bullet points, which coincide with the nine sections of the canvas:

- Channels; besides the social selling, new media channels can be useful for improving the engagement with your target market, keeping in touch with your customers, or simply promoting your products. Independently of what you are going to do, you need to choose which social networking sites are going to have presence on, and how you are going to develop it.
- Customer segments; it may be useful to know the profile of our target market, so we can choose accordingly the channels where the users do match better these profiles.
- Customer relationship; once generated a lead or generated the attention, how are you going to close the transaction? (online vs offline).
- Value proposition; which problem are you helping your clients solve?, what is making you different from the rest of the solutions in the market? Use social media to do your market research (i.e.great low-cost alternative to focus groups) and for customer service.
- Key resources; nowadays the war for talent can be won by using social media; create a brand as an employer, identify better candidates, improve the full employee's lifetime cycle.
- Key activities; did you know that social media can help you be a better project manager? (i.e.team communication).
- Key partners; social media can help you identify them, strengthen relationships, and improve collaboration efficiency.
- Cost structure; would the usage of social media channels help you save money?
- Revenue streams; will social media induce new sources of revenue increasing your turnover?

Finally, it is recommended you practice first with a well known model (would you be able to create the Business Model Canvas behind the series of games of "Angry Birds"?). Then, once you have got used to the canvas, try filling your current values considering no social media strategy to, at a later stage, complete the model with the social media bits. Moreover, it is going to be more dynamic and efficiency if you gamify the process: bring your team into a brainstorming session and build it together!

1.5 Things to do before writing your social media plan

I am sure that if you are initiating your journey along the social media realm, as user, client, or consultant, you have realised you need a roadmap. For those coming from the management world this is nothing new: every business strategy has to be made explicit in a document that is well known across the whole of the organisation.

Your digital strategy has to follow this same procedure. However, do not undertake this task as if it was a chore and then do it very leniently or without any preparation or, at worse, copying-pasting from a general template. The social media plan is going to govern your way into the social channels for the following 24 to 36 months, so you better get it right!

Then, once you have understood the importance of designing this digital strategy, I would like you to consider the main three considerations you will need to reflect on before starting writing your social media plan.

Which is the strategy of your organisation?

Social media has an strategic role, and the social media strategist or person in charge of developing the social media plan should be a person with ties to the Board and the executives in the company. You have to consider that the digital strategy does not have any sense if it is not aligned to the general company strategy. The lack of alignment could cause some problems in the deployment of the digital strategy: do we compete at national level or are we a global company?, are we the cheapest or the one with most quality in the market?, is our digital brand expressing the same values as the main corporate one?

It makes no sense to try designing a digital strategy if the company does not have a general strategy. However, trying to develop your social media plan may be the revulsive that enforces the design of a general strategy. If you need to design both at the same time, why do not try using the Balanced Scorecard?

Which is the marketing strategy of your organisation?

The same situation will be found with the marketing plan. You must know it really well before starting your social media plan. You should understand the marketing-mix strategy of your company. Do you get along well with the marketing department people? You better do! If you want to do a good integration of the social media strategy with the marketing strategy you will need not only to understand the marketing-mix, but to get the data that drives the marketing decisions.

The marketing-mix is a simplified model explaining which factors affect the marketing of a product or service. It was devised in the nineteen fifties as an easy way of generating marketing models. This model considers four factors that can be used to create a marketing strategy: price, product, promotion, and place.

- Price relates to the own price of the product or service, and it is the main factor of the four. For example, when setting a price a company should take into account which is the value prospective customers or users are going to get from the product, which is the competition average price, and so on. This is, a pricing strategy entitles a lot of different variables to take into account.
- Product factor considers the core characteristics of the product or service and which needs does fulfill, how different is from the competitors' offering, or which are the attributes that are valued by the customers or users. It comprises both tangible and intangible characteristics. As a whole, the product has to fulfill the

customers needs: what do they need?, when do they need it?, how much are they willing to pay for it?

- Promotion is about communication campaigns and word of mouth. It is about making sure that the target market will know the product or service. Further, the aim of promotion is to ensure they have a good impression of the brand and will end up buying. We are considering TV, radio, printed ads, direct marketing, cold calling, sponsorship...
- Place is about offering the product where the customer needs it and when it is needed. It relates to the sales channels and to the supply chain.

Since all four factors start with a letter P, the model is commonly known as the 4Ps of marketing.

Incorporating the social perspective into the price pillar of the marketing mix introduces new ways of analysing your pricing. The value proposition and the value generation comes from the whole of the organisation; every single member or function should be focused on either increase the perceived value or to reduce the cost, so then, increasing the value. However, it is the power of social media to increase the perceived value the one I would like to stress.

Social media can help you with your pricing strategies, too. Have you ever thought of testing different prices for your products? (supermarkets do this continuously). This is called A/B testing, and it is a practice that people from SEO and e-commerce do very often to check which words, designs, or layouts work best to convert visitors into customers. Guess what! You can do something similar using social media. Or, if you consider this might be too advanced or complicated, at least you will be able to use the social channels as your market research realm.

And with this market research and your different pricing strategies you could estimate the price elasticity of your demand. This is a concept that comes from economics, and which is related to how sensible is your customer to price variation. Again, you can try estimating it by using social media.

So does allow to experiment with different discounts and offers. The important thing when using any of those, as well as the previous tests, is to track for the differences in conversion. That's why we are introducing the concept of conversion funnel in the next subsection.

If the product factor considers the core characteristics of the product, when incorporating the social channels into the analysis we should think of the social recommendations. People are more and more getting used to comment into the social networks and give their opinions about everything (including your product).

Then, it is the figure of the prosumers: consumers or future customers that participate into the design of the product. We could consider him as a proactive consumer, although ultimately in the new economy the process of prosumption is the act of creation of products and services by the same people who will ultimately use them. Have you heard of wikinomics? (in line with this paradigm).

Market research and focus groups is another way of integrating the social factor into the product pillar of marketing-mix.

If we can summarise promotion as communication campaigns and word of mouth, when incorporating the social channels into the marketing mix model, we could resume it as lead creation and lead nurturing.

Inbound marketing is the new marketing paradigm as with promotion. While contents are the bait and search engine optimisation is what allows for our contents to reach our target market, social media is what amplifies our message. Blogs, ebooks, viral videos, podcasts, webinars, RSS and the like are the contents which will allow us to attract leads to our sales pipeline.

Although it may seem to be really new and trendy, one must remember that relationship marketing has been around for many years. This type of marketing focuses on customer retention and customer satisfaction, instead of stressing the close of sales transactions. However, as you can imagine, social media allows companies to strengthen the relationships with their customers, so then improving satisfaction ratings and reducing the churn rates: customers more satisfied and who stay as your customers for much long.

Both inbound marketing and relationship marketing have been linked to another concept, which we can call non-intrusive marketing. Social media allows brands to be discovered by the customers, rather than forcing the discovery. Good contents strategies and smart and pervasive usage of the social channels will make your brand easily discoverable and, from here, if you nurture your customers... voilà! Happy customers.

Further, if you acknowledge that new social responsibility relates to keep in touch with the people around your company, and being transparent. Why not using social media to do so? Yes, social media and promotion can be a powerful corporate social responsibility tool.

Finally, the place factor can be leveraged with channel optimization whenever we start considering the social channels.

E-commerce and f-commerce can make good use of the geographical segmentation. How the social networking sites are evolving, more reliable geographic information is being obtained from the social channels. From absolute position through GPS information, to geo-tagging, and geographic information induced from the own contents (for instance, users referring to their country, or the place they are commenting on) brands are being more and more capable of extracting further knowledge.

When including the people perspective into the marketing mix we obtain a new model. Make good use of it! The 5Ps model.

Do you know really well the sales funnel of your organisation?

As we have explained at the beginning of this chapter, every function in a company has to add value to increase the profits of the organisation. Further, it is critical the functions help increase the perceived value by the customer, since this will increase the price the customers are willing to pay for our product or service.

You must remember that I have made clear that you must focus on conversion. Why? Because companies succeed and remain active as long as they are capable of generating profits.

Due to the fact that we are considering the social media channels, then you should be focusing on social conversion: the process by which your activity in social media will aim to bring you new leads and will help you improve your sales.

Actually, the process is more complicated that this, due to the fact that we may consider many steps in what it is called the conversion funnel, so called the sales funnel

It is very important you are aware of the workflow of your sales/commercial process. Conversions are the fuel that lets a company to succeed and stand the pass of time. Without conversions a company would not be achieving its main targets (i.e. for a for-profit company, you get it, profits), and sales are the main driver for surviving in the long term. Having said that, you will need to have a very good relationship with the commercial department and/or the commercial director. Otherwise, you better start nurturing this relationship. Once you have analysed these three aspects of your organisation you should be able to start working in your social media plan: your digital strategy.

The sales funnel is based in the principle that the sales process follows several stages. First, the marketer needs to define which is the target market of the product, service, or brand that is offering.

- Awareness is when your target public gets to know your brand. This is, there is a percentage of the target market that converts into being aware of your brand, product, or service.
- Interest is the stage when a percentage of the people aware of your brand are interested on it. The conversion in this step means your brand is more likely to be bought because interest has been raised. However, there are still two other steps in the funnel.
- The next stage of the process is for this segment of the target market that is interested in your brand to Desire it. It is almost the final step in the conversion funnel. Between those who are interested in your brand only a percentage will be actually desiring to own it.
- And the final stage is when that desire converts into an Action, like buying the product or contracting the service. Other type of conversion rather than the purchase may be what it is known as "advocacy"; this is when the action is related to an act of defending or talking positively about the brand.

This model may be named according to the acronym A-I-D-A: the AIDA model.

Once you have understood how the sales funnel works you should be able to apply it to the social channels. Some argue that the AIDA model is not applicable to social.

However, this is quite wrong. The AIDA model does not need to be linear and unidirectional. You may adapt the model to transform it into a circular flow. In this new design, awareness, interest, desire, and action go in circles, in a no-ending flow.

In fact, we could consider further ties and connections between the different stages. Social media may alter the flow of relationships: for instance, allowing a percentage of the target market move from awareness to desire. However, we could argue that what it is actually happening is that social media is speeding up the whole process, rather than transforming it.

1.6 Marketing: expense or investment?

Do not lie to yourself, not every penny you invest in marketing and promotion is an actual investment. What's the difference? It is easy, if you spend your precious money in a marketing campaign and this provokes profit betterment, then that is well invested money.

> Half the money I spend on advertising is wasted; the trouble is I don't know which half
> John Wanamaker (1838– 1922)

So, let's consider the equation for marketing spent in marketing and promotion is 50% expense and 50% investment. What happened if I told you some analysts are capable of estimating which is the 50% that works? Furthermore, what if I told you that some techniques might even enlighten about which marketing campaigns and channels are better suited for improving sales, reducing operational costs, leverage up-selling and cross-selling practices or, alternatively, which ones have a better ROIM (Return on Investment of Marketing)?

There are multiple techniques that make good use of your sales data, connecting the dots between your core (financial) results and the several campaigns and marketing channels your company might have been using, even social media (i.e. does an increase in your Twitter followers or Facebook fans relate to your sales increase?).

Every action has an outcome..... or it should. Another of the sayings of management says that you cannot manage what you do not measure; that's it!, if you are unable to give an answer to the question "which are the outcomes of my business actions?" then you are not dealing responsibly with your business: you are not managing it.

The same apply to marketing, then. You must measure and monitor your marketing-mix (pricing policies, promotions, product development and offering, place), the actions associated to these and, mostly important, their outcomes. Once you have been able to find which are the best methodologies for measuring every marketing channel, linked to your marketing strategy, you will be able to assess your marketing performance (targets vs actual results).

Further, if your measuring activity is so effective that you are capable of connecting the cost of every channel with the derived benefits in currency terms, then you will know which channel has the biggest return on investment (ROI).

Please note the strength of that information: once you are aware of the ROI for every channel and activity, you will be able to optimise your marketing plan, relocating resources to the most profitable channels, your predictions on the outcomes of new campaigns will be more accurate, improving your budgeting, and you will have a better understanding of cause-effect within your marketing and business processes. So, are you willing to measure your marketing-mix ROI?

Chapter 2
Social Media ROI

2.1 Defining social media ROI

ROI is a financial concept that measures the net profit of a company, project or campaign generated in comparison with the invested costs. Sometimes it is called profitability; ROI is Return On Investment, the profitability of an investment. ROIM, another similar concept, is when we apply the concept of ROI to marketing. It measures the impact of marketing and communication on the company results. ROI is presented as a percentage indicating the net profit that has been generated from every invested dollar.

Actually, I prefer to use the term profitability. ROI is a comparison between the benefits and costs of a particular action: if the benefits outweigh the costs, bingo!, the action is profitable, otherwise, we say that the action is not profitable!. Therefore, what we are doing is subtracting the costs to the benefits to see if the result is positive or negative, indicating whether the action adds value (your profit, net profit, or margin) or destroys it.

NET PROFIT = BENEFITS– COSTS

One problem with this measure is that it can be misleading, since it does not allow us to compare: is 1,000 pounds a high or small amount? What if I say that you need to compare it with 1 million pounds? If I tell you your net profit is 0.1% of that 1 million pounds then this net profit is actually a very small amount.

The ROI of a campaign is calculated by dividing your net profit by the costs of this campaign, and multiplying it by 100. Thus the ROI tells you how many pounds you get of net profit per hundred pounds of cost.

ROI = [NET PROFIT / COST] x 100

And what about the term "social media ROI"? Many people get upset when I say this, others get angry, and some laugh: the ROI of Social Media is the ROI measurement when the campaigns to which we refer are social media campaigns. That is, when we measure the ROI of social media activities.

It is a measure which is easy to understand and indicates the success of a campaign, project or channel:

- A positive ROI shows that the campaign has generated more benefits than costs.
- A campaign with higher ROI indicates that it has been more successful than other one with lower ROI.

ROIM, another similar concept, is when we apply the concept of ROI to marketing. ROIM measures the impact of marketing and communication on the company results.

ROI helps us to compare the success of different campaigns, even when they are not from social media channels, or even when they are not from marketing and communication. For example, you can compare the ROI of a Facebook campaign with the ROI of employing another call-center operator.

There are other definitions for ROI that are not ROI strictly speaking: Impact on Relationships, Return on Participation, Return on Attention, Return on Trust, Return on Engagement, Return on Connections, Return on Interest, Return on Innovation, Return on Ignorance, Return on Involvement, Return on Interaction, Real Online Interaction, and maybe other concepts that I may have missed but that by no means are real ROI.

So, how can we fit those definitions with the real ROI?: actually, they are not alternative definitions but different concepts that try to compare the different benefits of social media from a qualitative perspective. While ROI measures as a percentage comparing costs and benefits in dollars, the other indicators do it qualitatively. But we can still use them: how? They are concepts that extract the benefits from social media, and that in the global company strategy help reach the target of ROI.

Anyway, real ROI will need to account for COSTS and BENEFITS. Then, apply the formula.

2.2 Why is so important to measure the ROI of social media?

I do not think you have to calculate the ROI of social media because it is fashionable; it would be stupid. You have to calculate the profitability of your social media campaigns because you have to know if they are being helpful to gain money or if you are wasting money.

The ROI of social media tells you if the cost of your investment in social media is generating you a profit or if it is hurting your finances. Even if you are not spending money, you think you are spending your time, and your time also has a cost: for example, rather than devote two hours a day to keep your social media presence, you might be serving as a barista, winning 20 pounds an hour. Indeed, if you invest your time social media can get benefits.

Nobody likes to lose money, but usually the amount of money devoted to social media is not very high compared to the budgets of other campaigns and marketing efforts. You should know if you are getting an adequate return on that investment, though. I can think of thousands of questions that can be answered by calculating and comparing the ROI data. Here are some:

- Interested in maintaining the investment in social media?
- Are your actions most profitable in Facebook or Myspace?
- Should you offer a promotional discount to existing customers of the physical store or reinforce your business on Twitter?
- Interested in advertising on the radio, or is it better to hire new creative designs for your social presence?

2.3 How to measure and calculate social media ROI

Measuring Social Media ROI, as it happens with the ROI of Marketing, is very complicated. Maybe that is why you will find on the internet countless people who either want to believe that you cannot (or should not!) measure it _as you could not measure"the ROI of a mother" or "the profitability of a hug"_ or have invented alternative metrics of dubious utility to determine if you are making or losing money with your campaign (i.e. Impact of Relationships, IOR).

The challenge is not in applying the formula we all know add, subtract, multiply and divide. Further, the difficulty is not in getting the costs information. The difficulty resides in obtaining the information about benefits.

If you want to estimate the ROI of your social media presence you need to calculate its benefits and the costs. While estimating the benefits attributable to social media is quite a complicated task, measuring the costs is not so difficult. What it is recommended though is you hand this over to your accountant so he will be able to give you advice on some of the concepts.

2.3.1 Costs in social media

Human resources

The first cost related to human resources you should consider is the initial consultation. If you are not a craftsman of the social media or do not have the time, willingness or enough knowledge to start a social media strategy, you will have to hire a skilled consultant.

As for the cost of starting a social media consultancy project, even if you can get an accurate quote, you should know that the amount will depend on the size of your project and the scope in which you want your brand to be developed. As you see, this will depend on your business model and how your value chain is structured. In addition, it will also depend on the reputation of the consultant.

Once you have started the project, the other major cost on the staff side will be the community manager. You must consider that this cost, unlike the consultancy one, will be incurred every month regardless of whether you decide that this person or team is internal or external. If you hire someone external, follow the same process you would use to hire a consultant. In fact, maybe your chosen consultant will recommend someone to perform such work in your community management tasks.

If you hire someone internal, calculate the costs based on the gross wages, national insurance contributions, and other personnel costs.

In this cost section, entrepreneurs or managing directors often forget to include the cost of their time. Have you considered that? Your time also has a cost: the opportunity cost. This is the cost of your time, measured as the amount you are missing because dedicating your time to the social media instead to other tasks, like selling, managing your business, or even leisure.

Technology

This is another important costs source. You probably do not need to buy a computer for community management, but whether you have had to buy it as if you are using what you already had, you should estimate the monthly cost attributable to social media. On the software side, nowadays there are many tools that allow you to manage and monitor your community. Usually there are good free options that allow you to manage your social networks in a very professional manner. Sometimes you will need to pay for the"pro" versions.

Other costs

Under this heading I include other costs you should consider: web design, images, infographics, logos, offline advertising (why not? Evangelise in the physical world and attract people to your community) and online (SEO/SMO, SEM/SMM), gifts and promotions, other costs associated with the activity (i.e. travel, training, lodging. . .).

Then, when you have calculated your starting up costs and your monthly costs you are ready to proceed with the next step to be able to calculate your social media ROI: the benefits.

2.3.2 Benefits of social media

Maybe you have heard many times that "social media are conversations" and that, consequently, they can not be attributed ROI because you cannot measure the benefits of your customers or users talk about your services or products, on your brand, or that it is impossible to measure engagement.

One reason why many people say that you cannot measure the ROI of social media is because people are unable to measure the benefits. I tell you now: it is possible, but it will not be easy.

Before listing the possible ways in which social media can generate profits, do not forget that social media is a marketing and communication channel. Although it is also true that social media is not a channel that should be treated the same way as the other channels.

Anyway, does TV have the same characteristics as external ads, or has radio the same features as a trade journal (to name a few)?

In addition to the interactivity of this new channel, you must keep in mind that:

- It is very dynamic.
- It is much faster and flexible process in which the transmission of messages, information and content are developed.
- It is rampant in many cases.

I will propose that from the foundations proved throughout the last decades using traditional channels, you should experiment to test what benefits can really bring social media to your company, brand or project. Here I propose you four aspects to which you should pay attention.

Social selling

When reviewing the benefits, in my opinion the most important will be the sales conversions. However you will need to analyse this for your own organization, since every company and strategy will have different targets and results.

Sales conversions will have to be evaluated using the "customer lifetime value" (CLV), that is the value your company will get from every customer while he buys from you. At the end of the day, we are aiming for obtaining customers that repeat purchases.

This would be a way of calculating the benefit coming from new customers. Calculate the "customer lifetime value", estimate how many new customers you obtained thanks to social media, and you can estimate the benefits of acquiring new clients.

From this perspective, you could argue that social media may allow you to increase the value of current customers. For instance, by increasing the margin, or their loyalty, which would increase the average customer lifetime.

Cost savings

Further, social media can help you save costs. Increased brand visibility is translated in cost savings in promotion and advertisement. Media equivalent value estimates how much have we saved by having had free impressions. We can calculate it multiplying the number of impressions by a theoretical CPM, plus total clicks times a theoretical CPC, plus total leads times a theoretical CPA.

Customer service 2.0 could be considered another source of cost savings. Effectively, call-center reduction usage is another source of cost savings. It measures the reduction of costs in the service of customer support through a call-center. It can be calculated by multiplying the number of contacts made by the social channels times the call-center contact cost.

Reduced costs in market research, since the interaction with the users in social media can provide with information on preferences, tastes, and opinions.

Savings in content generation (UGC, User Generated Content), if building a community is achieved and the users act as ambassadors of our brand.

Brand equity

Finally, improved online reputation management would be difficult to measure but it is still an important benefit computed as a cost avoidance (i.e. lost sales due to reputational crisis, consumer activism leading towards a boycott, etc).

Social media cannot only avoid worsening brand sentiment, but it may help to improve sales when the management has been done rightly. Further, as explained with the customer lifetime value, better branding will increase our margins and the loyalty of our customers, so then increasing the conversion benefits.

Chapter 3
Measuring Social Media ROI

3.1 Three concepts for mastering social media ROI measurement

You have probably read many myths and legends (and many lies as well) around the concept of ROI. However, it is not necessary to reinvent the wheel. This time I'll tell you what three questions or tools you have to keep in mind to run away from the myths that have been created around social media ROI.

At the beginning of every science there is a red thin line between what it is considered science and what is alchemy. For example, we all know Isaac Newton as the first scientist, when he should be more famous for being the last alchemist. Why social media ROI should be different from physics?

Fortunately, more and more consultants, academics and practitioners of this fantastic profession of digital marketing and communication are abandoning alchemy and necromancy, the dark arts of social media. If you want to join us and want to master social media ROI measurement, take care of these three concepts.

3.1.1 Causality vs chance

If I kick you in the leg and it hurts, it is very clear that there is a direct relationship: there iscausality. If you read this post and your leg hurts. . . .. yes, it's coincidence (chance).

In our terms, if a social media campaign has been brutally successful in terms of'likes', 'followers' and other non-financial indicators (soft indicators, opposite to the hard ones, or financial and commercial), it does not mean you are getting a good ROI. Neither the fact that you are growing your soft indicators while the hard ones are also improving has to indicate the existence of a causal link; yes, it may be pure chance (again!).

Human beings are naturally selfish, and maybe some egocentric. The social media manager may think that all the increase in sales is attributable to the social media campaign, without considering if there have been other campaigns (i.e. offline media), changes in the rest of the marketing mix, or other competitor activity that may have affected the sales.

Regardless, if you want to measure the possible existence of causality, you can start with the most common and easy to calculate statistical measurement: the correlation coefficient. However, detecting correlation does not imply causation; resorting to the correlation coefficient is only an initial technique to try to conclude whether the evolution of the soft impact on financial indicators is significant. How? If there is no correlation, you can assure there is no causality,so then concluding the lack of it. Otherwise, you should start analysing if the detected correlation may come from a causation or mere chance.

3.1.2 Marketing-mix (again!)

Price, product, promotion, and point of sale: in the twentieth century, a basic marketing model allowed that with only four groups of determinants explain how a product or service differentiated from other competitor products.

How does social media fit into this model? Very easy, by incorporating a fifth P: people. You should be able to assign the strategies and actions to each one of the pillars of the marketing mix. Moreover, it is possible that you have been explained the model of the four Cs (hey, there are many, I mean: Clients, Content, Context, Channel), indicating that this is better because it is consumer-oriented. I do not like it, because it focuses too much on the communication processes, when social media can aspire to much more than being simply channel of communication and relationships with the users/clients.

If you really want to set aside a model with more than fifty years of existence because you consider it obsolete, something I disagree with, then you can use the model of the four Cs of the nineties: Cost (instead of Price), Consumer (instead of Product), Communication (instead of Promotion), and Convenience (instead of Point of Sale). While you were reading the C-words have you been able to visualise your Community (instead of People)?

3.1.3 Sales funnel

The target market for your products and services can be considering many consumers. However, only a percentage of it will know about your products, and only a small part will be interested in them. Of the later group, a few will buy or use your service.

This process can be represented by a funnel, known as the sales funnel, and it can be easily remembered by the acronym AIDA:

• Awareness (of your brand)

- Interest (on your product)
- Desire (want your product)
- Action (purchase it)

This funnel is similar to that one used by SEOs and web analytics professionals, but you will have to consider that not only from online sales business thrive, and that there are many businesses out there that sell physical products in physical stores. Those must also measure sales, although the process will be more difficult.

Once you have understood the three concepts and how they relate to social media, you will be ready for social media ROI measurement, since we are gradually assembling the puzzle that is taking us to know how to calculate it.

3.2 Social selling: a new customer journey?

Do you think social networks have changed the way you sell? Can you take advantage of them in your daily life?

Although social networks have changed the sales process from a business perspective and marketing, if you understand well what place in that process you will become a very useful tool to change some processes.

Why do I focus on sales if I'm talking about social media and it still has to prove conclusively that it can become a successful sales channel? Well, it is clear that a company survives because it sells its products or services, therefore every activity a company does must be geared toward the sale (please, do not confuse this with wishful thinking!).

> Very briefly: if you do not sell, do not invoice, and if you do not invoice….. the company disappears.

No wonder why I recommend you to run away from those who instruct you to engage in just getting and measuring followers, likes, RTs, etc.

Forget it! Every action should be directed towards achieving the sale. And because of that you must focus on your sales funnel.

Traditionally, the sales cycle has been represented as a funnel, because what happens from one phase to another is that the percentage of the target market you capture is diminishing.

Therefore, the graphic form gives the impression of a funnel. However, many other models have arisen, even representing marketing and sales as a continuous loop, representing the consumer journey as a non-stop process.

The truth is that many believe that social media has changed the sales funnel because it can allow customers and users to bypass stages, going back and forth in the funnel, there are processes of attracting new customers, etc.

Well I don think it is changed that much! Have they not understood that a model is a simplified representation of reality? As well as there are many possible cases being able to be explained by a single model? Did not social relations exist before social networking sites?

The sales funnel is still able to explain all of these situations, but the complexity is higher for several reasons:

- Increased speed and dynamism of actions (buying and selling, interactions, comments, complaints.....).
- More data that should be analysed.
- More channels on which to attribute a conversion.

But being more complex does not mean that the model is no longer useful, just have to know how to adapt. Indeed, social media may have had a profound effect on the sales cycle. However, before stating that the sales funnel has changed is trying to change quantum mechanics.

Choose the best model that fits your universe. Perhaps you do believe that social media is able to change the laws of physics, when you are really failing is with the application of the equations.

Before social media, many of the movements in the sales cycle and effects originated and caused situations that reinforced (or detracted) marketing strategies and alter the flow of the sales cycle occurred.

What is happening now is that social networks (humans) have become more powerful, thanks to the effect of social networks (tools). Nothing has changed, only the speed at which things happen. Do you use social media in your measurement model? Are you aware of how they affect your sales cycle?

3.3 Are you converting social leads into sales?

Why is it so hard to measure your actions in currency in the social networks? Can you measure the online conversions? And when they convert into offline sales? You know that it is possible to measure social media ROI into your offline sales? There are a number of techniques that can help you narrow in what you do offline sales in social networks. But how?

Do you turn fans into buyers?

Let me emphasise the importance of the sales funnel and how this concept is related to conversion. That is, if you know how your users react to your actions and activities of marketing and communication, you can maximise your investment and get better results. For example:

- Is it better for you to focus on Facebook and forget about Twitter?
- Is it worth you make a contest on Pinterest?
- Can you afford to hire a Community Manager or is it better to invest that money in discounts and promotions?

Where is the real problem?

Unfortunately, a number of problems that prevent conversion rates get measured exactly, or even not being able to be calculated in any way. This could happen, inter alia, by:

1. Online; multi-channel conversion. In an online business, are sales made solely on the last click, or rather depend on a process that finishes with the last click? What if this process took place over several days, not only at the time of purchase?
2. Offline. A large percentage of sales could happen through offline channels (i.e. in the case of physical stores).

You need to identify all the actions to see how all the players react along the pipeline from becoming a lead to the final sale. And that is not an easy task. So here I leave a number of strategies that will help your sales be effectively measured and you will be able to evaluate the profitability of your actions on the social networks:

- Use affiliate marketing (remember that this type of marketing existed even before the internet!); affiliate programs, clicks on banners, coupon codes, cookies...
- Use correlation techniques; search for statistical evidence of correlation between social indicators and financial and commercial indicators.
- Ask your customers; how they decided to buy from you?, through which channel?

3.4 The social media ROI KPI you cannot forget

Do you know that there is a key indicator for Social Media ROI you should always have in mind? Do you want to learn how to calculate the value you obtain from your clients from social networks?

As I explained about the theory of the value chain, all roles in the company must contribute to increase the value added of the organization and, more importantly, the perceived value to the customer. As long as the customer perceives more value in your product or service, the greater the likelihood that buys from you, that when he buys he will remain your client, and that he is willing to pay the price.

So if you understand that social media is a powerful tool to increase the value of your brand and a channel to improve profitability, you have no excuse to stop reading this.

ROI is a financial concept that measures the net benefits to a company, project or campaign generated compared with the costs that have been invested. That is, you must not only take into account the costs of your business, but also the benefits. And this is where our key indicator comes into play.

All your activities, not only in social media, should focus on conversions. Conversion is the process through which users or consumers from your target market become aware of the existence of your brand until they continue or end their relationship with it; remember the AIDA model. This model is known as the sales funnel, where the aim is sales and subsequent actions, such as the defense of the brand (Advocacy) that certain users do on social networks, or the generation of content (UGC, User Generated Content).

And at this stage is when our key indicator comes into play, being this key indicator the Customer Lifetime Value (CLV). The client, after making the first purchase until he leaves us, makes a series of repeated purchases. CLV is a concept that every financial department and every sales manager should be calculating, and know that it represents the income that a client will provide the company during his whole cycle.

Although the calculation of CLV can be quite complicated for the information you need, having to use financial formulas, and making certain decisions, you can actually calculate it in a simple way if your sales process is not so complicated and your customer cycle is not so long.

CLV = ARPU x ACL

- ARPU (Average Revenue Per User) is the average revenue per user, which can easily calculate by dividing net sales by total customers or users. Actually, it would be much more convenient to use the AMPU (Average Margin Per User), but I understand that to obtain this information can be sometimes more complicated.
- ACL (Average Customer Lifetime) is the average life of the customer, and represents the average time that a customer is one. As you know, customers come and go, and after a first purchase is not going to repeat all or repeat all that they will do so indefinitely. This is an indicator that is linked to customer loyalty, and you can calculate it as $100/CR$, where CR (Churn Rate) is the percentage of customers who each time period (month, week, day) cancel their contract.

Well, you have learned how you can start measuring the ROI from an important part of your social media activities; if you are able to measure the number of new customers that you have obtained through Social Media, multiplying this figure by the CLV you will get the value gained from social sales. And there's more: since one of the benefits of social media is to use the social channel as a loyalty tool, if you achieve this objective, it will be reducing the CR (alternatively, increasing the retention rate), which will be increasing the ACL and ..... voilà!, improving the CLV.

Of course, I am not saying that social selling and the effects of social media over sales are going to be the only ones so making the positive returns of social media solely reliant on sales. I do acknowledge that many companies are obtaining cost savings on the customer care side of social media, and others still consider advertising value equivalency to be a good benefit from social media exposure. But, while you analyse, measure, and calculate your own Social Media ROI... let's consider CLV your best bet.

Chapter 4
Conclusion: Social Media ROI in 30 sentences

1. Understand Social Media ROI. Social Media ROI is the financial return of your activity on social media.
2. Understand the ROI of Marketing. In marketing and communications, ROI has been measured from a long time ago: ROIM (ROI of Marketing).
3. Express it as a percentage (%). ROI is an indicator measured in percentage, calculated from the comparison between measured costs and monetary benefits.
4. Know the ROI equation. Social Media ROI equation is: ROI = [(Benefits - Costs) / Costs] x 100 = [Net Income / costs] x 100
5. Know what the % ROI indicator means. ROI in percentage tells you how much money you have earned (net) per each dollar that you have invested in the activity.
6. Measure your costs and benefits. Social Media ROI can be measured, but it requires measuring the costs and benefits; as some benefits are intangible, they are difficult to measure. But it is not impossible: everything is measurable.
7. Measure the ROI of all channels. There are stubborn people wanting you to measure the ROI of social media when they have never considered measuring the ROI of other channels, whether online or offline.
8. Learn to differentiate between what is ROI and what it is not. There are people saying you cannot measure social media ROI, others say you should not even try it! Some people even invent new ways to measure ROI... but what they measure it is not actual ROI, since they do not express the outcome in currency.
9. Simulate scenarios. You cannot measure Social Media ROI before you start a project, action or campaign. However, in any case you can estimate it or perform a scenarios simulation.
10. Learn finances. To measure social media ROI properly you need to have basic knowledge of finance, business, strategy, marketing and communications, not just Social Media!
11. Know your costs. To measure the ROI of Social Media you need to know your costs.
12. Focus on key cost drivers. You can focus on the 3 main areas: human resources, technology, and other operating costs.

13. Measure your human resources costs. These are the costs of consulting, training, start up, the community manager's salary and, do not forget, your time.

14. Measure the cost of your time. Possibly, the cost of your time is the most difficult part to measure; use the concept of opportunity cost (ie, how much you would earn if you dedicated your time to other tasks).

15. Measure your technology costs. These are generally less important. You already have a computer, and the monthly cost for the necessary software tools to manage and monitor social media are usually inexpensive; it is even possible that the free versions serve you.

16. Measure other costs. When evaluating other operating costs you should not forget the costs of content generation, online and offline advertising, and you might want to generate community using competitions.

17. Calculate the costs. Time and technology are relatively easy to estimate. The costs related to human resources can be obtained through quotes, market reports or asking to your colleagues for benchmark data.

18. Invest in a good community manager. A cheap community manager can be expensive. Remember: pay peanuts... (get a social media crisis!).

19. Perform cost scenarios. If you estimate an a priori Social Media ROI, it is convenient to work with several possible costs. For example, a mean value and a range between +/- 20%. Although costs are usually quite clear and certain, and there are no major changes, double-check your numbers and analyse them by doing scenario analysis.

20. Differentiate between cost and investment. Finally, once you have had all the estimated costs, ask yourself: is this cost going to help generate profits? If the answer is "yes" then it will no longer be a "cost", but an "investment". Remember the third word in ROI is "investment" (Return on Investment).

21. Know the benefits of your actions. To measure the ROI of your actions you need to know the benefits achieved with them. These benefits must be measured in the same unit you measured your costs: currency (ie. dollars).

22. Focus on three measurement areas: customers, cost reduction, and brand equity.

23. Understand the benefits associated to customers. Social media may be attracting new customers and improving sales, and/or profit margins on existing customers (cross-selling, up-selling). Know your conversions and the customer life-time value.

24. Measure the cost reduction. Social Media can help you reduce costs, which is also a benefit that you should measure.

25. Understand cost reduction measures. Some cost cutting measures are customer care (ie. savings linked to customer service 2.0), improved internal communication costs, or savings in market research.

26. Measure the intangibles, like improved brand equity, which can also be measured in currency. It is difficult, but still could be performed.

27. Consider the right benefits. You should only consider those benefits where there is a clear relationship between your social media actions and the benefit.

28. Identify the benefits. To help you in the task of identifying benefits you can use the sales funnel, because it will force you to closely monitor your sales. Using

the coefficient of correlation you can check if there is evidence of causality (ie. social actions producing higher sales volume).

29. Estimate profit scenarios. As with costs, it is convenient to work with ranges of possible values. In the case of benefits, since some values are approximate (ie. intangibles), when calculating the ROI of an activity you should be working with different scenarios.

30. Use measurement methodologies. There are no point-and-click tools that measure your ROI automatically; you must estimate your values for each case, and these calculations require collecting several amounts of data. I am aware there are methodologies that apply average values, or benchmark values. Be careful and use the data in your industry and/or product... but with care. You should always aim to get your own calculations.